The city after quarantine

Imagining the anarchist city
in times of empty streets

CoCo — cooperativa conjunts

Authors:
Belando Morant, Marta
Calle, José Antonio
Jiménez, Fabiola
Espinoza Díaz, Kleber
Kuzmanic, Jere
Simons, Daniela

Design and layout
Robles Sosa, Alejandra

Written: May 2020
Revised: November 2021

The manuscript of this text won the best manifesto award at the TU Delft Summer School Planning and Design for the Just City. A shorter version can be found at:
Rocco, R., & Newton, C. (2022). A Manifesto for the Just City, Volume 2 (Vol. 2). Delft: TU Delft ABIERTO.
Both volumes of manuscript collections are available for free download. On the TU Delft Online Book Catalog:
Volumen 1 (2020) "A Manifesto for the Just City: Cities for all" DOI: 10.34641/mg.14
Volumen 2 (2021) "A Manifesto for the Just City : 2021 edition" DOI: 10.34641/mg.36

The cities and regions of the world are on hiatus. We have little time and much to do. The COVID-19 pandemic can be a test of what awaits us and that is why we need people who are informed, organized and willing to build our present and future hands-on.

This text is born of the desire to make visible how we could change the inertia of the established social order that will collapse sooner rather than later, being aware that the new paradigms, this time, will have to be based on social and environmental justice. We understand this crisis as an opportunity, chaos as a gift offering to understand life as a constant rhythm construction-destruction and that any process of growth has an implicit error, therefore making transformation inherent to all natural cycles. The pandemic is a trigger for new ways of living, planning and imagining cities as a symbiosis of many living organisms within a physical environment.

The following lines are an open manifesto in which the individual's freedom within the inherited planet is valued without question. This collection of dreams for the future is an anarchist act of call to cooperation for all those people who wonder about the possibility of living in a balanced world with values such as horizontality, mutual support, empathy, solidarity and autonomy and that denounces the aggression between us and over the biophysical environment we inhabit.

Content

CHANGE OF THE STATE OF EMERGENCY FOR THE STATE OF CARE.

THE CONTEXT IN TIMES OF HEALTH CRISIS OR BEFORE

"'Normality' in itself is a crisis. We need to catalyze a massive transformation towards an economy based on the protection of life". Words of Naomi Klein (2020) show that the current health crisis adds to the ecosocial crisis that we are experiencing and has only pointed out what activities are necessary to sustain life.

Even more so, before confinement, the culture of care was already in our DNA, be it as the defence of the quality of our public health or through informal neighbourhood networks of mutual support. These days, due to the urgent need, even more groups emerged to facilitate the day to day of the most vulnerable people. Through assistance to people at risk, gathering protective material for the health sector, food for people who cannot afford it, free taxi services to hospitals... Streams of care spread among the neighbourhood beyond what we could have imagined before March 2020. The undervaluation and low remuneration of reproductive work, linked to the sphere of care, has been made visible, unlike in pre-pandemic 'normal' times, when productive work, linked to sometimes unnecessary goods and services, enjoyed high salaries and social recognition.

PROPOSAL:

As citizens, we want to know what role cities play in supporting the ties of mutual help and care work when it transcends the family sphere or network. As Jane Jacobs pointed out, relationships on the street or in a local community can develop people's attachment to where they live; therefore, also to the neighbourhood of which they are part. It seems that way how we build environment has lost sensitivity for the relationships between the people and has simply been designing spaces of isolation -many times without flexibility in the face of the different profiles of homes that exist today-, with little communication with the street life and with a spatial configuration that embodies a sexual division of labour -as its hierarchical design does not have a neutral meaning-; all this favoured by the regulators themselves.

The most widespread models for the distribution of housing, such as buying or renting, have excluded many people from the right to decent housing. However, many alternative models challenge the private property system and favour community participation in caretaking, reproductive labour and shared health. An example is the cooperative housing in the cession of use, or the agreements through the so-called "masovería urbana", even the squatter movement, which carries the full weight of these experiences.

Cities can care, and we can take care of ourselves in cities, appealing to a balanced distribution between genders and the valuation of the time dedicated to care, from the logic of being eco-dependent and interdependent as defended by ecofeminists. Greater neighbourhood interaction, with community support networks favoured through the design of common and community-made spaces, including community-made green spaces such as allotment gardens, provides a sustainable vision that can transcend all scales of habitability.

ACTION STRATEGIES DURING AND AFTER QUARANTINE:

- Be aware of the hours we spend on care work (at home and away) and try to balance them
- Find out about the social groups in your neighbourhood and participate in the one we feel most comfortable with
- Knowing our neighbours by name, helps to create links
- When possible, encourage gathering in public spaces by creating safe and welcoming spaces

Illustration
Adolph Kruhm

REVALUATION OF THE NATURAL LANDSCAPE IN CITIES

THE CONTEXT IN TIMES OF HEALTH CRISIS OR BEFORE:

We have dysfunctionally shaped the planet's surface, destroying the native landscape to build cities, unrooting primary forests and thousands of wildlife habitats to create solid blocks that arise from the surface, imposing, noisy and dirty. When did we start to prefer the sound of a car over the singing of birds? The pandemic is a Trojan horse for nature to reenter the city. We see animal species reclaiming the streets that we did not see before in urban environments. This forces us to reflect on how we have exploited other living beings' to preserve our own. When we re-territorialize ourselves in the environment and slow down our mechanisms of 'development', the richness of life grows and balances itself again. The 'empty streets' reveal the condition we have subjected nature to for as long as we call it modernity. The apparent void of development is an opportunity for introspection on how we have created cities and urban regions, these spaces that we believe belong to us, while they are home to infinites of wild species and miracles of life that make possible our tenancy of this Planet.

PROPOSAL:

The Garden city by Ebenezer Howard is an urban idea designed for a healthy life and work, with a size that makes possible a full social life, but in a controlled sprawl, surrounded by green belts and rural landscapes as biological corridors that allow synergy with wildlife (Howard, 1989). This new ecological and metabolistic urban landscape will emerge from understanding energy flows and the entropy of those that are productive to find an economy allied with nature allowing us to take advantage of its resources in a sustainable way without endangering the life conditions of others.

One thinks of the concept of the garden city as proposed by Howard, replacing industrialized production with multi-skilled citizens that work together in small hi-tech workshops and orchards. And a large city where the micro-centres of urban life make possible plural autonomy while well connected with the environment including the peripheral mosaic of agricultural soils. Aren't the city and the countryside

Kupari, Croatia 2021
Photo by
Alejandra Robles Sosa

Illustration
Désiré Bois
supposed to function as a single integrated system?

ACTION STRATEGIES DURING AND AFTER QUARANTINE:

- Map places where we can stock up on local produce.
- Get organized with more people and occupy free spaces in the city where we can cultivate.
- Engage in local planning processes demanding different paradigm (i.e. Garden City)
- Learn about the geography of our local surroundings: bio-regional, hydrological

and information on land-use   history of our area

TOTAL FUSION OF CITIES AND NATURE, FOR A REPRODUCTIVE CITY, NOT EXTRACTIVE

THE CONTEXT IN TIMES OF HEALTH CRISIS OR BEFORE:

The biggest problems we face in this health crisis are caused by the shadow behind it; anthropocentric social metabolism. The construction of society is based on creating an empty comfort at the cost of the destruction of natural resources that ensure our survival. The anthropocentric system links "basic needs" to individualised benefit, violating the minimum conditions of collective well-being.

Trapped in this conception of "mine", we manufacture an excessively processed and plastic life. We buy packed fruits in a supermarket, we break the link between the product and its origin, disconnecting human activity from the natural environment.

We develop structures that generate marginalisation in the social and physical environment, blindly protect profitable financial entities, and minimise common welfare. Countless examples are out there in which human economic activity violates life. The lack of protection of life and neoliberal practices linked to anthropocentrism facilitate a series of comforts that do not ensure the adaptability and resilience of human life.

PROPOSAL:

Let's plan cities and regions as physical biocultural/interactive/ natural systems, grouping these attributes and selecting solutions that dismantle the dichotomy between the flows of the city and nature. Understanding the existing interdependencies at both social and natural relationships, we must create layers of knowledge, let us be guided by a single frame of reproductive socio-natrual interaction, and formulate city models that respond to the context of needs and available resources, setting limits of the growth.

Therefore, we ought to develop regional planning that creates models of interaction between the landscape and the people who inhabit it. The strategies need to be worked on at all scales to transform cities from their current anthropocentric operation of extraction and exploitation of resources, species and fellows towards one that reproduces resources in tight relationship to their regional and metabolic surroundings and social ties. For urban planning, the flow capacity that the environment possesses must be a foundation on which cities can regenerate within the larger territory they are interconnected with and the socio-environmental dynamics that maintain

Drvar. Bosnia and Herzegovina 2021
Photo by
Alejandra Robles Sosa

these in balance. It could start with the decarbonisation of the economy and changes in supply chains that drive the transportation models, food production, and energy consumption.

ACTION STRATEGIES DURING AND AFTER QUARANTINE:

- Find out about, promote and get involved with community groups and cooperatives that seek to build new models of coexistence with non-human world
- Reduce or avoid buying items/goods that are unnecessary
- Consume ecological and local products, in which it is ensured that in their manufacture and production, there is a minimum impact on the environment.

NO GREENWASHING, NO SPECULATION, NO GLOBAL COMPANIES, NO MASS TOURISM, AND NO SUBORDINATED LIVES

THE CONTEXT IN TIMES OF HEALTH CRISIS OR BEFORE:

Life on Earth depends largely on regenerative processes within a finite planetary system, and this is why we cannot afford to extract non-renewables endlessly. The cities play a part in consuming this capacity by expanding land-use patterns, increasing consumption and pollution. This is because they are built in the paradigm of the perpetual pursuit of (economic) growth.

The imperative of economic growth is deeply rooted in the contemporary notion of well-being (i.e. green growth, sustainable development goals). It is believed that socio-economic development cannot be sustained without 2-5% economic growth per year. The pandemic of COVID-19 made especially visible the limits of this economic model; it is unstable and not very resilient. The movements of degrowth and buen vivir highlight the social and environmental harm of the growth model and reframe human progress along the lines of regeneration and conviviality.

Within these perspectives, we could imagine multiple benefits of the COVID induced slowdown, from the absence of tourists in the city centres to skies empty of restless flights. However, it is important to bear in mind that what is happening is not degrowth or buen vivir but a demonstration on a global scale of the possible limits that society can impose if it recognizes that the regeneration of the natural system is a priority over the growth of the economy.

PROPOSAL:

Degrowth establishes two parallel and at first sight contradictory objectives: to develop the economy so that it does not exceed the planetary system's limits and simultaneously distributes social justice and a basic quality of life to all living beings. The contradiction is resolved by dismantling the relationship of growth and development, and in words of Giorgos Kallis making room for concepts to imagine and promote diverse futures that share the objective of reducing the scale of affluent economies and their material flows, in a fair and balanced way (Kallis, 2015). What does this mean for cities?

The many existing degrowth-oriented practices are already working on this transition; urban gardens, autonomous communities, cooperative housing, food banks... These proposals are the seed of degrowth that we are looking for in cities.

However, their impact is limited. They are often unsystematic and demanding examples of incredible collective and personal effort that find no way to persist at the city or district scale. To imagine the future of a territory based on degrowth, different scales of self-governance should emerge: from neighbourhood assemblies and local action groups, to the scale of mass blockades of construction sites and extraction facilities, ZADs and TAZs, "hacking" the institutions and dismantling their ties with global corporate enterprises, boldly implementing city-scale commons and squatting professional discussions to implement limits on the expansion of motorized traffic, mass tourism, or urban sprawl. There are many options.

ACTION STRATEGIES DURING AND AFTER QUARANTINE:

- Read literature on degrowth and buen vivir
- Track and trace large scale businesses and their spatial facilities.

Try to understand how their business influences your environment.
- Think about how we can travel without using tourist facilities

and cheap flights. Think about the ways green can become political-join the public debate with degrowth arguments.

- Engage with local action groups, ZADs and environmental activists.
- Connect with the local degrowth community.

COMMONING THE LAND, FOR THE REGION AS A HOME WITHOUT HIERARCHY AND EXPLOITATION

THE CONTEXT IN TIMES OF HEALTH CRISIS OR BEFORE:

Urban planning has lost the battle while quantifying land, distances and feasibility. Rural life, nature, and the countryside have a purpose for the human being in contemplation, health and above all, freedom. This might be why lately more criticism of the city can be heard, such as that they are too big, unkind, dirty, polluted, segregated, and dangerous. Faced with the health crisis, we have confined ourselves, closing the doors of housing, shops, and borders. Nevertheless, out there, spring has arrived, and the cities stood under clean blue skies, exuberant vegetation, and the flux of fauna roaming the streets. We gave more value than ever to the outside, to the contact with nature and the societal dimension of the natural environment.

The crisis and recession are concepts implemented in a model of society that only speaks of development in terms of growth and profit. The greatest crisis is the one that our flood of consumption causes today.

As we face the perfect storm, a multidimensional 'crisis'

Kupari, Croatia 2021
Photo by
Alejandra Robles Sosa

Illustration
Charles Morren

(economical, energetic, ecological, and health), we should rethink the foundations of how our society is functioning and our relations with the territory. Increasing biodiversity and organic agriculture, ecological urban and rural relations, common goods, the right to the city and countryside, food sovereignty, and resilience could become strategic aims. We must claim the future of a balanced region.

PROPOSAL:

The ability to produce local food should be one of the main variables to be considered to achieve a change in the patterns on which the supply of cities is based and even further, for a radical turn of the tide in how people relate to their surroundings and themselves. We propose to recover the land lost after industrialization as a communal natural right, to reconquer the soils and voids as available for common use, agriculture and resource management. These relationships between eco-urban and rural areas should improve through commoning, taking advantage of voids in consolidated and unconsolidated urban land, in suburban areas and ecotones.

By recovering the lost communal territory, we will be able to find ways to supply energy, water, and food to the users. And with planning actions done in a specific way all the inhabitants will be able to adapt with equal opportunities and responsibilities. Possibly, more social cohesion will occur as people will cherish their renewed contact with the region and countryside.

We should take part in building together planted, rural, public, common, and private spaces since all can support social relationships and improve their sense of belonging on many scales.

ACTION STRATEGIES DURING AND AFTER QUARANTINE:

- Find available spaces where we can cultivate to achieve relative self-sufficiency in our own home: a window, a balcony, a empty plot in your neighbourhood, a terrace, a square
- Team up with our neighbours to promote a system of urban gardens and water harvesting, which we can all take care of, exchange seeds, and plant trees and herbs
- Travel to the countryside as often as possible, walk, cycle, eat in the local taverns and squares
- Educate ourselves about a biodiverse future, regionalist movement and skills of living with and taking care of the nature
- Get involved in local political movements to defend, expand and radicalize local environmental and territorial politics

CORE VALUES OF THE POST-CAPITALIST CITY

THE CONTEXT IN TIMES OF HEALTH CRISIS OR BEFORE:

France is known as the country of "thousand kinds of cheese". French could have a different cheese for dessert every day of the year without repeating the same. It is not the result of hazard but the consequence of a social context and historical events. The wisdom says that the "cheeseversity" that we have today is due to the Black Death epidemics that ravaged Europe in the second half of the fourteenth century.

The isolation of cities and regions to protect themselves from the virus implied a reduction in trade and exchange of raw materials. Thus, cheesemakers were forced, on the one hand, to implement recipes using those ingredients and gadgets that were available at the local level. On the other hand, the difficulty of exporting the cheeses outside the local scale forced them to improve conservation and curing techniques that would allow them to be available for selling and eating for a longer time.

Therefore, looking at history shows the fragility of the prevailing economic system faced with crises that escape mathematical predictions of the market. Indeed, economic growth implies having a constant increase in consumption. For consumption to increase, greater competitiveness is required, improving the performance of the product offered or optimising production costs. Then, increasing specialisation is required, for both, people in individual labour, and territories in productive activity.

From neoliberalism's point of view, in the ever more connected world, the economy has to grow and, therefore, crystalise and individualise social fabric, generating a society that depends on globalisation but not on the skills of a fellow neighbour.

Limited mobility means social interaction limited way below our emotional needs. This has been magnified by the post-industrial fabrics of our cities and territories through zoning and land use regulations, specialising vast areas into one purpose deserts. The urban space responding to the capitalist dynamics has only aggravated its weaknesses in the face of crises such as the ones we are experiencing today and those to come, such as climate change.

PROPOSAL:

As the current pandemic shows, the system can avoid collapse only by applying the opposite principles to those applied by neoliberal doctrine. It is on whom we depend in the face of the crisis that has to be reconsidered. On the one hand, the intense economic exchange is incompatible with the social isolation required by the pandemic. But, on the other hand, specialisation has made us utterly dependent on others, causing an immense surge of immediate non-profitable local cooperation and mutual aid.

Indeed, as a society, it is necessary to cooperate in mutual support. We had to change our habits and economic dynamics to build more cooperative societies and innovate new ways of living and working in order to overcome the pandemic as a new socio-economic condition. Looking at the past could give us the answers how to maintain society under such terms: self-help housing,

Segal Close, United Kingdom 2021
Photo by
Jere Kuzmanic

workers support funds, planning aid groups, community land trusts and voluntary action societies that build autonomous, self-sufficient and mutually supported neighbourhoods and workplaces into federations of collaborating cities thanks to nowadays available communication skills and information technologies. That is the only way we could keep enjoying a good tasting cheese.

ACTION STRATEGIES DURING AND AFTER QUARANTINE:

- If we have a job for bare financial stability: In general, we won't have enough time to change our ways of organizing. However, we will maybe have some economic profit to change our consumption habits. Support a cooperative business and ethical financial bodies.
- If we do not work and are economically vulnerable: We will not have money, but we will have time to change our habits. Get connected into the social fabric of mutual support. Time is the currency we can exchange for the support of others. Join street kitchens, food deliveries and eviction defenses.
- If we do not work, but have financial stability: We are in a perfect situation to change both our consumption habits and ways of organizing. Initiate and organize cooperatively, be a pioneer, consider joining a housing cooperative or turning our source of financial stability into a

- cooperatively run enterprise.
- If we have a job, but we are economically vulnerable: Unfortunately, we will not have time to change ways we organize or economic margin to change our consumption. Keep our trust in society. Let the support get to us through solidarity: at work (unions and workers trusts), at streets (food banks, communal gardens), at home (health aid, intergenerational support groups)

SELF-DEFENCE AGAINST THE IMPERIALIST POLICE, ARMY, MACHISMO AND THE SECURITY SYSTEM BASED ON FEAR

THE CONTEXT IN TIMES OF HEALTH CRISIS OR BEFORE:

One of the most important ingredients for the COVID-19 cure is collective responsibility. Collective implies the shared trust and confidence that people understand the danger and respect distances, protective measures, and the need to act responsibly. It applies not only to strictly staying home but also to behaviour in public spaces, when with family, friends, and neighbours. Different countries have different measures for distributing responsibility among their citizens, and precisely this has an extended impact on the outcome of the crisis.

Let us take the spanish state as an example. After the first psychological shock of restricting any movement, when people understood the level and scale of the danger, something went wrong in how the state addressed this collective responsibility. Images of the police threatening and beating people alone in the streets, the army patrolling urban areas with weapons, restricting jail visits, detaining those without papers, war narratives on television...

What was the message of these government actions? We do not trust you. We have to centralize responsibility because distributed responsibility does not work. In terms of numbers but also in psychological terms, the consequences are to be experienced later. The dependence of states on violence and the priority of their monopoly to exercise it over the ability of people to understand, change behaviour, be respectful, or simply intelligent is not exclusive to the crisis. It is a common mechanism of all authority. The monopoly of violence is the persecution the state and capitalism will sustain when everything collapses, and the strength of this monopol will increase over time.

PROPOSAL:

This will simply not change. The institutions that constitute the monopoly of violence (the police, the army, the legal and prison system, heteropatriarchy, and Westernism) are the most difficult to imagine disappearing from contemporary society. The state and capitalist society will not shoot a bullet in their own leg. Neither will we, as people and popular movements, commit ourselves to do so without knowing the result. Self-defence is the first step to ensure respect between the institutions of violence, the state, and the people. Before erasing them, we have to be respected for the power we possess in numbers and intelligence. Collective responsibility has to come from below, from trust among people, from solidarity, and from a shared belief in the possibility of justice.

Imagine a concept of justice based on healing instead of punishment. The community surrounds the culprit and tells each other what good this person did apart from the criminal act until the person feels like part of the community again. This could be a basis for restoration of mutual trust and a collectively shared sense of justice. This will never be a dimension of our society until we win the respect of the monopolists.

ACTION STRATEGIES DURING AND AFTER QUARANTINE:

- Look from our balcony and window, take care of our neighbours and how the police treat them on the streets
- Engage in groups and communication channels that are monitoring it on the level of neighbourhood or city. Talk about collective responsibility with our closest ones
- Once the quarantine is over, engage with prisoner support groups, for example, send books, join the anti-military or self-defence group in our city
- Never join the imperialist army or advocate war for state or capital

THE FUTURE IS NOT FOR SALE. NO ONE HOMELESS, EVERYONE STATELESS

THE CONTEXT IN TIMES OF HEALTH CRISIS OR BEFORE:

Waking up in a state of emergency and curfew confronts us with the sense of lost freedom. It forces us to spend days and nights in our homes, those static spaces in which we usually voluntarily develop a large part of our lives. These often happen to be the only pixel of lived space under our control. The remaining space is shaped by a totalitarian model of state or whatever authority and with pandemic it reveals true flaws in the face of the support for the basic needs of world's inhabitants.

Throughout history, those settlements that grew in population had increased fear of pests resulting in protocols and facilities to provide complete isolation. The exclusion of the contaminated was total, as it was of the community towards the outside. This sense of control contributed to developing the attraction towards the possession of 'space' or land where one or a few

Mostar, Bosnia and Herzegovina 2021
Photo by
Alejandra Robles Sosa

had everything needed. With time we inscribed this attraction in our society and cadasters. Property gives many promises: security, social status and economic possibilities to turn land into money.

Wealth in properties gave some the power to control and discriminate, which divided the territories and led us to a surreal geopolitical fragmentation in which we believe we have to take part. That need to control and feel safe in our cities does not guarantee us the necessary resources to survive as pandemics showed, so the question arises, What is ours? And, what is the use of control over land?

PROPOSAL:

We shall no longer consider ourselves an inhabitant of a home, city, or country as a territory of exclusion, even more, the owner of any pride in that. Think of a place where one can develop their way of living in a group with no control over land and living space via power but through cooperation, where they cultivate the collective before the individual modes of (n)ownership. Letting go of the power and wealth accumulation for the abundance of sharing will give meaning to our shared lives and give new types of relationships that we form as a society and within the environment. As bold as it is, this proposal is the essence of

spatial and environmental injustice on all scales. Property is theft.

The speculators and landlords live from the land that belongs to everyone. They create money adding artificial exchange value to a common good that has endless use value and that simply can't be commodified. We should not take part in this senseless economical fraud and instead work on deliberating as much land and homes as possible for a wide range of inhabitants including non-human. The possession should essentially come with shared responsibility towards the accessibility and reproduction of the space and not with the privilege of earning money on other people's work in capitalist trap. All land is ours and all land can be managed as commons. All humans need a home and home is more than just a private roof over one's private head. That home can be built, maintained and possessed as a shared space of many purposes for many users with models such as community land trust, self-help housing schemes and back-to-the land occupations of capitalist wet dreams such as airport extensions, open mines and speculative housing estates.

ACTION STRATEGIES DURING AND AFTER QUARANTINE:

- Catalogue what activities we have stopped doing and note which ones we would stop since we now believe they are unnecessary

- Observe what we do not use, and that may be useful to another person to allow us to detach ourselves from it and share it

Collage by
Alejandra Robles Sosa

Illustrations
Friedrich Losch
Varignana F. Mitelli

- Read and understand the injustices of land and tenure, ownership and the way it inscribes injustice in space
- Start a group with our friends to discuss how we want to live when we get old and how do we see our vision of the world of no man's land

RE-TERRITORIALIZATION AND INDIGENOUS CULTURAL RESISTANCE. RESPECT EXISTENCE OR EXPECT RESISTANCE.

THE CONTEXT IN TIMES OF HEALTH CRISIS OR BEFORE:

New sunsets with returning migratory birds, scenes of a spontaneous play of sea animals that were never seen before on the coasts give us hope these days that we can live in a more inclusive world. The unexpected rehabilitation of ecosystems besieged us as spectators of processes that we had stopped observing due to speed and our attachment to an individualistic life that constantly demands more from us.

This new moment to contemplate the void and the decrease in movement in our cities without anyone roaming and enjoying them makes us think about the value of the things that we have gained and lost in our personal and collective history. Everything we have built in contemporary civilization is based on a western and colonial idolatry of a sudden and quick gain of wealth and accumulation. Some deserve more than the others because they work, exploit or loot more.

It is why, according to Thomas Moore, utopia is the only tool that allows us to imagine. Let us not forget that nowadays, as well as during the large part of history, exist indigenous societies that preserve and maintain territories, integrating natural cycles and knowledge into their way of life, and in which we can still trust and whose ways we can still revalue before we spoil them. Imagine a world according to their ways.

PROPOSAL:

Submission to an established structure omits other perspectives and histories. We can unwesternize how we live with our territories and decolonize how the west relates to indigenous cultures and ways of inhabiting the Earth since the current capitalist way of life has determined subsistence on this planet in totalitarian absoluteness.

Our ancestral civilizations and cultures often were based on knowledge and beliefs that value beings on Earth holistically, be it plants or animals, therefore they kept a knowledge of living in harmony with the environment for thousands of years. And a large part of this memory is preserved by indigenous societies around the world. We, who failed in this, have to learn the fundamental importance of coexistence and learning empathy for the other through respecting the struggle to reclaim a sense of belonging to all those nativities we stripped of the future a long time ago. Because coexistence is, as our ancestors and native predecessors knew, not inscribed in the map but in vital cyclical flows of earthly life.

ACTION STRATEGIES DURING AND AFTER QUARANTINE:

- Learn the meaning of the term decolonize and support the movement of indigenous people towards their autonomy
- Think less about ourselves and what we miss and make an effort to start taking care of what we have inherited.
- Slow down and introspect to recognize what beings we live surrounded with. See how similar and different we are to them and how much we are willing to share with everyone around us.

**Guna Yala, Panamá 2016
Photo by
Alejandra Robles Sosa**

**Illustration
Mich Detroit**

"Cuando sueñas solo,
sólo es un sueño;
cuando sueñas con otros,
es el comienzo de la realidad"

Proverbio Brasileño

"When you dream alone, it is
just a dream. When you dream
with others it is the beginning
of reality"

Brazilian proverb

La ciudad después de la cuarentena

Imaginamos la ciudad anarquista en tiempos de calles vacías

Cooperativa conjunts

coco

cuarentena

Autores:
Belando Morant, Marta
Calle, José Antonio
Jiménez, Fabiola
Espinoza Díaz, Kleber
Kuzmanic, Jere
Simons, Daniela

Diseño y maquetación
Robles Sosa, Alejandra

Escrito: Mayo 2020
Revisado: Noviembre 2021

El manuscrito de este texto ganó el premio al mejor manifiesto de la TU Delft Summer School Planning and Design for the Just City y en una versión más corta se puede encontrar en:

Rocco, R., & Newton, C. (2022). Un Manifiesto por la Ciudad Justa, Volumen 2 (Vol. 2). Delft: TU Delft ABIERTO.

Ambos volúmenes de colecciones de manuscritos están disponibles para su descarga gratuita. On the TU Delft Online Book Catalog:

Volumen 1 (2020) "A Manifesto for the Just City: Cities for all" DOI: 10.34641/mg.14

Volumen 2 (2021) "A Manifesto for the Just City : 2021 edition" DOI: 10.34641/mg.36

Las ciudades y regiones del mundo están en pausa. Tenemos poco tiempo y mucho que hacer. La pandemia de la COVID-19 puede ser un ensayo de lo que nos espera y por eso necesitamos personas informadas, organizadas y dispuestas a construir desde la práctica nuestro presente y futuro.

Este texto nace de la voluntad de visibilizar cómo podríamos cambiar la inercia del orden social establecido que colapsará más pronto que tarde, siendo conscientes que los nuevos paradigmas, ahora sí, van a tener que basarse tanto en la justicia social como en la justicia ambiental. Entendemos las crisis como oportunidades, en que el caos se presenta como regalo para entender que la vida se basa en una construcción-destrucción constante y que el crecimiento tiene implícito el

error, por eso la transformación es inherente en todos los ciclos naturales. La pandemia juega un papel importante como detonante de nuevas formas de vivir, de planificar e imaginar las ciudades como una simbiosis de organismos vivos con el medio físico.

Las siguientes líneas son un manifiesto abierto, en el cual se valora la libertad del individuo sobre cualquier sistema heredado sin cuestionamientos. Esta colección de sueños para el futuro es un acto anarquista de llamado a la cooperación para todas aquellas personas que se preguntan la posibilidad de vivir un mundo pacífico con valores como la horizontalidad, el apoyo mutuo, la empatía, la solidaridad y la autonomía, denuncian la agresión entre nosotros y la ejercida al entorno biofísico que habitamos.

Contenido

CAMBIAR EL ESTADO DE EMERGENCIA POR ESTADO DE CUIDADOS.

CONTEXTO EN TIEMPOS DE CRISIS SANITARIA O ANTES:

"La 'normalidad' es una inmensa crisis. Necesitamos catalizar una transformación masiva hacia una economía basada en la protección de la vida". Palabras de Naomi Klein (2020) evidencian que la actual crisis sanitaria se suma a la crisis ecosocial que vivimos, y no ha hecho más que señalar qué actividades son necesarias para el sostenimiento de la vida.

Fruto de ello, antes del confinamiento, la cultura de los cuidados ya estaba en nuestro ADN, sea desde la defensa a la calidad de nuestra sanidad pública o mediante redes informales de barrio de apoyo mutuo. En estos días, debido a la urgente necesidad, han surgido grupos que facilitan el día a día a las personas más vulnerables, mediante asistencia a personas de riesgo, material de protección para el sector sanitario, alimentos para gente que no puede pagarlos, servicio de taxi gratuíto a hospitales... Redes de apoyo que se han extendido entre el vecindario sin que nos lo pudiésemos imaginar antes de marzo de 2020. Se ha visibilizado la infravaloración y la baja retribución del trabajo reproductivo, ligado a la esfera de los cuidados, en una situación de 'normalidad' pre-pandemia, mientras el trabajo productivo, ligado a bienes y servicios a veces innecesarios, gozaba de altos salarios y reconocimiento social.

PROPUESTA:

Como ciudadanía queremos saber qué papel juegan las ciudades para favorecer lazos de ayuda mutua y que los trabajos de cuidados trasciendes incluso el ámbito o red familiar. Como indicaba ya Jane Jacobs, las relaciones en una calle o en una comunidad local pueden desarrollar el apego de las personas al lugar en el que viven; por tanto, también al vecindario del cual forman parte.

Parece que el entorno construido haya dejado de lado las relaciones entre las personas, y simplemente se haya encargado de diseñar espacios aislados, -muchas veces sin flexibilidad ante los diferentes perfiles de hogares que existen hoy en día-, con poca comunicación con el exterior y con una configuración espacial que

plasma una división sexual del trabajo -ya que su diseño jerárquico no tiene un significado neutral-; todo ello favorecido desde la propia normativa.

Los modelos para disponer de vivienda más extendidos como son la compra o el alquiler, han dejado fuera del derecho a una vivienda digna a mucha gente. Sin embargo, existen multitud de modelos alternativos, que ponen en cuestión el sistema de la propiedad privada y que favorecen la participación y salud comunitaria. Un ejemplo son las viviendas cooperativas en cesión de uso, o los acuerdos mediante la llamada "masovería urbana", incluso el movimiento okupa, que lleva todo el peso de estas experiencias.

Nos pueden y podemos cuidar las ciudades, apelando a un reparto equilibrado entre los géneros y la valoración del tiempo dedicado a los cuidados, desde la lógica de ser ecodependientes e interdependientes como se defiende desde los ecofeminismos. Una mayor interacción vecinal o de barrio, con redes de apoyo comunitarias, favorecidas mediante el diseño de espacios comunes y comunitarios, incluyendo huertos comunitarios, aporta una visión sostenibilista que pueda llegar a trascender a todas las escalas de la habitabilidad.

Ilustración
**Peter Henderson
& Co.**

ESTRATEGIAS DE ACCIÓN DURANTE Y DESPUÉS DE LA CUARENTENA:

- Ser consciente de las horas que dedicas al trabajo de cuidados (en casa y fuera) e intenta equilibrarlas.
- Informarse de los colectivos sociales que existen en tu barrio y participar en el que te sientas más cómodo/a.

- Conocer a tus vecinos y vecinas por su nombre, ayuda a crear vínculos.
- Cuando se pueda, fomentar la reunión en los espacios públicos creando espacios seguros y acogedores.

REVALORIZACIÓN DEL PAISAJE NATURAL EN CIUDADES

CONTEXTO EN TIEMPOS DE CRISIS SANITARIA O ANTES:

Equivocadamente hemos moldeado la superficie del planeta, destruyendo el paisaje natural para construir ciudades, desplazamos bosques primarios y miles de vidas silvestres, para crear bloques sólidos que se levantan en la superficie, imponentes, ruidosos y sucios. ¿Cuándo empezamos a preferir el sonido de un coche sobre el canto de los pájaros?

La pandemia es un caballo de Troya para que la naturaleza tome la ciudad. Vemos conviviendo en las calles especies de animales que antes no veíamos en entornos urbanos. Esto nos obliga a reflexionar sobre cómo hemos exterminado la vida de otros seres vivos para intentar preservar la nuestra. Cuando nos alejamos del entorno y desaceleramos nuestros mecanismos de "desarrollo", la riqueza de la vida vuelve a crecer y toma de nuevo el control. Las "calles vacías" delatan la condición a la que hemos sometido por años a la naturaleza. El aparente vacío de desarrollo es una oportunidad de introspección sobre cómo hemos creado las ciudades y regiones urbanas, estos espacios que creemos que nos pertenecen y que eran el hogar de cientos de especies silvestres que hacen posible nuestra estancia en este planeta.

PROPUESTA:

El Ciudad jardín de Ebenezer Howard es una zona urbana diseñada para una vida saludable y de trabajo; con un tamaño que haga posible una vida social a plenitud, pero de crecimiento controlado, rodeada por cinturones vegetales y comunidades rurales, que funcionan como

CDMX, México 2022
Foto de
Alejandra Robles Sosa

corredores biológicos y que permiten la sinergia con la vida silvestre (Howard, 1989). Este nuevo escenario ecológico tendría como bases el entendimiento de los flujos energéticos y de la entropía de los procesos productivos para encontrar una economía aliada de la naturaleza que nos permita aprovechar sus recursos de una manera sostenible sin poner en peligro las condiciones de vida de los demás.

Se puede pensar en el concepto de ciudad jardín propuesto por Howard, sustituyendo la producción industrializada por una ciudadanía con múltiples habilidades que trabaja conjuntamente en pequeños talleres y huertos. Asimismo, sustituyendo la gran ciudad por microcentros que están en sintonía con el entorno y con los suelos de producción agrícola. ¿No se supone que la ciudad y el campo funcionan como un solo sistema integrado?

ESTRATEGIAS DE ACCIÓN DURANTE Y DESPUÉS DE LA CUARENTENA:

- Mapear lugares donde puedas abastecerte de productos locales.
- Organizarse con más personas y ocupa espacios libres de la ciudad donde poder cultivar.
- Participar en procesos locales de planificación que exigen un paradigma diferente.
- Aprender sobre la geografía de tu entorno local: bioregión, hidrología o sobre la historia del uso de la tierra.

FUSIÓN DE LAS CIUDADES Y NATURALEZA, CIUDAD REPRO- DUCTIVA NO DE EXTRACCIÓN

CONTEXTO EN TIEMPOS DE CRISIS SANITARIA O ANTES:

Los mayores problemas que enfrentamos debido a la crisis sanitaria, son causados por la sombra que se encuentra detrás; el metabolismo social antropocentrista. Esa construcción social que se basa en crear una comodidad vacua, a costa de la destrucción de los recursos naturales que aseguran nuestra supervivencia. El sistema antropocentrista vincula las "necesidades básicas" al beneficio individualizado, vulnerando las condiciones mínimas de bienestar colectivo.

Atrapados en esta concepción de lo "mío", fabricamos una vida excesivamente procesada y plástica, compramos en un supermercado frutas emplasticadas, rompimos el lazo entre el producto y su origen, desvinculando la actividad humana del entorno natural.

Desarrollamos estructuras que generan la marginación del entorno social y ambiental, protegiendo a las entidades financieras, sobre la biodiversidad y el bienestar común. Se pueden mencionar infinidad de ejemplos en los que la actividad económica humana vulnera la vida. La desprotección de la vida y las prácticas neoliberales vinculadas al antropocentrismo, facilitan una serie de comodidades que no aseguran la adaptabilidad y resiliencia de la vida humana.

PROPUESTA:

Planifiquemos las ciudades y regiones como sistemas físicos-bi-oculturales- interactivos-naturales, agrupando estos atributos y seleccionando soluciones de máximo beneficio, para desmontar la dicotomía entre los flujos de la ciudad y la naturaleza. Entendiendo los vínculos existentes tanto a nivel de relaciones sociales, como naturales, debemos crear capas de conocimiento, para orientarlas en un cuadro único de interacción, para poder formular modelos de ciudades que respondan al contexto de las necesidades y los recursos disponibles, planteando límites de crecimiento.

Por lo tanto, debemos desarrollar una planificación regional que genere modelos de interacción entre el paisaje y las personas que lo habitan. Las estrategias necesitan trabajarse en todas las escalas, para lograr una transformación de las ciudades desde su funcionamiento antropocentrista actual de extracción y explotación de recursos, hacia una que reproduce sus recursos y cierra ciclos. Desde la

planificación urbana se debe valorar el grado actividad y movilidad que posee el entorno, para que las ciudades puedan regenerarse dentro del territorio y las dinámicas socio-ambientales que las mantienen en equilibrio. Se podría comenzar con la descarbonización de la economía y los cambios en las cadenas de valor; transporte, alimentación, energía, para darle forma a los espacios e interacciones humanas desde una aproximación equilibrada con el sistema ecológico.

ESTRATEGIAS DE ACCIÓN DURANTE Y DESPUÉS DE LA CUARENTENA:

- Informarse, promover e involucrarse en colectivos y/o cooperativas de proximidad, que busquen construir nuevos modelos de convivencia.
- Reducir y/o evitar comprar artículos/bienes que sean innecesarios.
- Consumir productos ecológicos y de proximidad, en los que se asegura que en su fabricación y producción existe un mínimo impacto al medio ambiente.

SIN GREENWASHING, SIN ESPECULACIÓN, SIN EMPRESAS GLOBALES, SIN TURISMO MASIVO Y SIN VIDAS SUBORDINADAS

CONTEXTO EN TIEMPOS DE CRISIS SANITARIA O ANTES:

La vida en la Tierra depende en gran medida de procesos regenerativos dentro de un sistema finito, y es por eso que no podemos darnos el lujo de extraer recursos no renovables constantemente. Las ciudades juegan un importante papel mediante el cambio de uso del suelo, el aumento del consumo y de la contaminación. Esto se debe al paradigma de búsqueda contínua de crecimiento. Uno de los motores clave de estas dinámicas es la perpetua búsqueda del crecimiento económico.

El "imperativo de crecimiento económico" está profundamente arraigado a la noción contemporánea del bienestar (es decir, crecimiento verde, objetivos de desarrollo sostenible, etc). Se tiene la creencia que sin un crecimiento económico del 2-5% por año, el desarrollo socio-económico no puede sostenerse. La COVID19 visibiliza los límites de este modelo económico;

inestable y poco resiliente. Los movimientos decrecentistas y del buen vivir resaltan el daño social y ambiental del modelo de crecimiento y plantean el progreso humano en la línea de la regeneración y la convivencia.

Podríamos imaginar pues, múltiples beneficios de la desaceleración de ciertas economías inducida por la COVID; desde la ausencia de un sinfín de turistas en el centro de la ciudad hasta cielos vacíos de vuelos inquietos. Sin embargo, es importante tener en cuenta que lo que está sucediendo no es un decrecimiento de la esfera material de la economía, sino una demostración a escala global de los posibles límites que la sociedad puede imponer si reconoce que la regeneración de los sistemas planetarios son una prioridad sobre el crecimiento de la economía.

PROPUESTA:

El decrecimiento establece realmente dos objetivos paralelos y a primera vista contradictorios: desarrollar la economía para que no exceda los límites del sistema planetario y que simultáneamente distribuya justicia social y calidad de vida básica a todos los seres vivos. La contradicción se resuelve, desmantelando la relación del crecimiento y el desarrollo y abriendo espacio a conceptos para imaginar y promover futuros diversos que comparten el objetivo de reducir la escala de las economías afluentes y sus flujos materiales, en una manera justa y equilibrada (Kallis, 2015). ¿Qué significa esto para las ciudades?

Las numerosas prácticas existentes orientadas al decrecimiento ya trabajan en esta transición; huertos urbanos, comunidades autónomas, viviendas cooperativas, bancos de alimentos. Éstas propuestas son la semilla del decrecimiento que estamos buscando para las ciudades. Sin embargo, su impacto es limitado y a menudo son ejemplos no sistemáticos y que demandan de un increíble esfuerzo colectivo y personal que no encuentran formas de crecer a la escala de ciudad o distrito. Para imaginar el futuro de un territorio basado en el decrecimiento deben existir diferentes escalas de auto gobernanza: desde iniciar asambleas vecinales y grupos de acción en el barrio, hasta manifestaciones masivas o el "hackeo" de instituciones y desmantelar sus lazos con empresas corporativas globales, implementando audazmente los bienes comunes a escala de la ciudad y ocupando los discursos con el objetivo de implementar límites en la expansión del tráfico motorizado, el turismo masivo o la expansión urbana.

ESTRATEGIAS DE ACCIÓN DURANTE Y DESPUÉS DE LA CUARENTENA:

- Leer sobre decrecimiento y buen vivir.
- Seguir a las grandes empresas y tratar de averiguar cómo su negocio influye en tu entorno.
- Pensar cómo puedes viajar sin utilizar las facilidades turísticas y vuelos baratos.
- Pensar en las formas en las que lo ecológico puede convertirse en política y unirse al debate político.
- Conectar con la comunidad local decrecentista.

COMO UN SISTEMA SIN JERARQUÍA Y EXPLOTACIÓN

CONTEXTO EN TIEMPOS DE CRISIS SANITARIA O ANTES:

La vida rural, la naturaleza y el campo, gozan de ciertos privilegios para el ser humano en contemplación, salud y sobre todo libertad. Sin embargo, las críticas hacia la ciudad aumentan cada vez más, y escuchamos que las ciudades son poco amables, sucias, contaminadas, segregadas y peligrosas. Ante la crisis sanitaria nos hemos confinado, cerrando las puertas de la vivienda, los comercios y las frontera. Afuera ha llegado la primavera y las ciudades muestran cielos limpios y azules, vegetación exuberante y el aumento de fauna recorriendo las calles; y nosotros le damos más valor que nunca al exterior, al contacto con la naturaleza y al acercamiento social.

Entendemos que las bases de nuestro modelo económico no son viables, que la crisis y la recesión son conceptos que se han venido implantando como un hecho recurrente en un modelo que sólo habla de crecimiento, que la mayor crisis es la que provoca hoy nuestra falta de consumo.

Nos encontramos ante la tormenta perfecta, una crisis multidimensional (económica,

Segal Close, Reino Unido 2021
Foto de
Jere Kuzmanic

Collage
Alejandra Robles Sosa

energética, ecológica y sanitaria) que nos obliga a replantear las bases del funcionamiento de nuestra sociedad y las relaciones con el territorio. El aumento de la biodiversidad y el incremento de la agricultura ecológica podría presentarse como un elemento estratégico cuando se vincula con las relaciones ecourbanas y rurales, bienes comunes, derecho a ciudad, soberanía alimentaria y resiliencia... debemos reivindicar el abastecimiento en cualquier futuro de región equilibrada.

El urbanismo ha perdido la batalla al cuantificar las reservas de suelo. La capacidad de producir alimentos de proximidad debería ser una de las principales variables a contemplar para conseguir un cambio en los patrones sobre los que se sustenta el abastecimiento de las ciudades, así como para el diseño de cualquier estrategia de transición hacia sociedades realmente sostenibles.

PROPUESTA:

Buscamos alcanzar un sistema de relaciones entre autosuficiencia funcional y metabólica del ecosistema con el territorio. Se propone recuperar el terreno perdido después de la industrialización como derecho natural comunal, reconquistar las tierras y los vacíos disponibles para uso común, agrícolas y/o ganaderas. Estas relaciones entre área

eco-urbana y rural deberán mejorar, aprovechando vacíos en suelo urbano consolidado y no consolidado, en zonas suburbanas y ecotonos.

Al recuperar el territorio comunal perdido podremos buscar maneras de abastecer de energía, agua y alimentación a los usuarios, planificando actuaciones de forma específica para que las estrategias sean adoptadas por todos los habitantes o de igualar oportunidades y reducir las brechas.

Naturalmente el incremento de la cohesión social no será una sorpresa, las personas se verán favorecidas al contactar con grupos con quienes pueden relacionarse, se deberá actuar en espacios rurales, públicos, semipúblicos y privados ya que todos tienen potenciales de establecer relaciones sociales y mejorar el manejo de recursos y desechos. Y la persona es el objeto central de estos espacios al vivirlos y apropiarse de ellos.

ESTRATEGIAS DE ACCIÓN DURANTE Y DESPUÉS DE LA CUARENTENA:

- Encontrar espacios disponibles donde puedas cultivar para alcanzar el autoabastecimiento en tu propia vivienda: una ventana, un balcón, una terraza o una plaza en tu barrio.
- Unirse con el vecindario para fomentar un sistema de huertos urbanos y recolección de agua, del que puedan hacerse cargo entre todos, intercambiar semillas y plantar diferentes especies.
- Proyectarse hacia un futuro biodiverso, en el que logres vivir en equilibrio con el medio natural.
- Implicarse en la política local para exigir cambios en la gobernanza.

VALORES CENTRALES DE LA CIUDAD POST–CAPITALISTA

CONTEXTO EN TIEMPOS DE CRISIS SANITARIA O ANTES:

Francia es conocida como el país de los mil quesos. Un francés podría comer cada día del año, como postre, un queso distinto sin llegar a repetir. Esto no es fruto del azar sino consecuencia de un contexto social y acontecimientos históricos. Cuenta el mito que la "quesodiversidad" de la que disponemos hoy en día es debida a las epidemias de peste negra que asolaron la Europa de la segunda mitad del siglo XIV. El aislamiento de las ciudades y regiones para protegerse del virus implicó una reducción del comercio y del

Segal Close, Reino Unido 2021
Foto de Jere Kuzmanic

Collage
Alejandra Robles Sosa

intercambio de materias primas. Así, los queseros se vieron obligados, por un lado, a implementar recetas haciendo uso de aquellos ingredientes y artilugios de los que disponían en la escala local. Por el otro, la dificultad de exportar los quesos obligó a implementar técnicas de conservación y curación que permitieran disponer de ellos durante más tiempo.

Es así, mirando la historia, como se demuestra la fragilidad del sistema económico imperante ante crisis que se escapan de lo matematizable. La lógica del capitalismo se basa en el crecimiento de la economía. Una economía va bien siempre que ésta crezca. Y entrará en crisis cuando decrezca.

Que haya crecimiento implica que tiene que haber un aumento del consumo. Para que aumente el consumo, se requiere una mayor competitividad, que mejore las

prestaciones del producto que se ofrece. Y para mejorar dichas prestaciones, se requiere una especialización cada vez mayor, que centre a cada cual en una tarea cada vez más específica, tanto a cada individuo en una tarea individual, como a cada territorio en una actividad.

PROPUESTA:

ACon la actual pandemia, el sistema sólo ha podido evitar el colapso desde la aplicación de principios opuestos a los que aplica la doctrina neoliberal. Es necesario reconsiderar nuestra capacidad de resiliencia frente a futuras crisis. Por un lado, el intenso intercambio económico es incompatible con el aislamiento social que exige la pandemia. Pero, por otro lado, la especialización nos

Es así como aumenta el flujo de intercambios, siendo éste, desde el punto de vista del neoliberalismo, el único camino por el que la economía puede crecer y, por tanto, mejorar. Esto ha generado la cadena mundial a la que llamamos globalización.

ha hecho totalmente dependientes de los demás, provocando una inmensa oleada de cooperación local inmediata y no lucrativa y de ayuda mutua.

Es necesario promover la cooperación y el apoyo mutuo como sociedad. Tenemos que cambiar nuestros hábitos y dinámicas económicas para construir más sociedades cooperativas e innovar nuevas formas de vivir y trabajar para superar la pandemia

Costa Rica, 2017
Foto de
Alejandra Robles Sosa

como una nueva condición socio-económica. Mirar al pasado podría darnos las respuestas sobre cómo mantener la sociedad bajo tales términos: viviendas de autoayuda, fondos de apoyo a los trabajadores, grupos de ayuda para la planificación, fideicomisos de tierras comunitarias y sociedades de acción voluntaria que construyen barrios y lugares de trabajo autónomos, autosuficientes y mutuamente apoyados. Actualmente tenemos las herramientas de la tecnología en comunicaciones para convertir las ciudades en federaciones colaboradoras. Solo así podríamos seguir disfrutando de un queso con buen sabor.

ESTRATEGIAS DE ACCIÓN DURANTE Y DESPUÉS DE LA CUARENTENA:

- Si tienes trabajo y estabilidad económica: Por lo general, dispondrás de poco tiempo libre para cambiar de hábitos. Sin embargo, quizás tengamos algún beneficio económico al cambiar nuestros hábitos de consumo. Apoyar un negocio cooperativo y organismos financieros éticos.
- Si no trabajas y eres vulnerable económicamente: No dispondrás de dinero, pero si de tiempo para cambiar tus hábitos. Conéctese al tejido social de apoyo mutuo. El tiempo es la moneda que podemos cambiar por el apoyo de los demás. Únase a las cocinas callejeras, las entregas de alimentos y las defensas de desalojo.
- Si no trabajas, pero tienes estabilidad económica: Estas en una situación perfecta para cambiar, tanto tus hábitos de consumo como nuestras formas de organizarlo. Inicia y organiza una cooperativa, emprende, considera unirte a una cooperativa de vivienda o convertir nuestra fuente de estabilidad financiera en una empresa administrada cooperativamente.
- Si tienes trabajo, pero eres vulnerable económicamente: lamentablemente, no tendrás ni tiempo para cambiar forma de organizarnos, ni margen económico para cambiar tu consumo. Mantener nuestra confianza en la sociedad. Que el apoyo nos llegue a través de la solidaridad: en el trabajo (sindicatos y patronatos de trabajadores), en la calle (bancos de alimentos, huertas comunales), en el hogar (ayuda sanitaria, grupos de apoyo intergeneracional).

AUTODEFENSA CONTRA LA POLICÍA, EJÉRCITO IMPERIALISTA, MACHISMO Y SISTEMA DE SEGURIDAD BASADO EN EL MIEDO

CONTEXTO EN TIEMPOS DE CRISIS SANITARIA O ANTES:

Uno de los ingredientes más importantes para la cura del COVID-19 es la responsabilidad colectiva. La amplia confianza de que las personas entienden el peligro y respetan las distancias, las medidas de protección y la necesidad de actuar responsablemente. Esto no se aplica únicamente quedándose en casa rigurosamente, sino también con el comportamiento en el espacio público, cuando se está con la familia, amigos y vecinos. Diferentes países tienen distintas medidas de distribuir la responsabilidad en sus ciudadanos y exactamente esto tiene un largo impacto en el resultado de la crisis.

Tomemos al Estado Español como ejemplo. Después del primer shock psicológico por la restricción de cualquier movimiento, cuando las personas pudieron entender el nivel y la escala del peligro, después de esa primera semana algo salió mal. Las imágenes de la policía amenazando y golpeando a personas solas en las calles, luego el ejército patrullando las zonas urbanas con armas, restringiendo visitas para encarcelar, deteniendo a aquellos sin papeles y narrativas de guerra en la televisión.

¿Cuál fue el mensaje con estas acciones del gobierno? No confiamos en ti. Tenemos que centralizar la responsabilidad porque la responsabilidad distribuida no funciona. En términos de números, pero también en términos psicológicos que nos enseñará las consecuencias después. La dependencia de los estados de violencia y la prioridad de su monopolio para ejercerla sobre la capacidad de las personas para entender, cambiar de comportamiento, ser respetuoso o simplemente inteligente no es exclusiva de la crisis. Es un mecanismo común de toda autoridad. El monopolio de violencia es la persecución que sostendrá el estado y el capitalismo cuando todo se venga abajo y aumentará su intensidad con el tiempo.

PROPUESTA:

Esto no cambiará simplemente.

Las instituciones que componen el

> "There is no forgiveness when someone who claims superiority falls below the standard."
>
> – Frantz Fanon, Black Skin, White Masks (1952)

monopolio de violencia (la policía, el ejército, el sistema jurídico y penitenciario, el heteropatriarcado y el occidentalismo) son las más difíciles de imaginar que puedan desaparecer de la sociedad contemporánea. El estado y la sociedad capitalista no se disparará una bala en su propia pierna. Tampoco nosotros, como personas y movimientos populares nos comprometeremos a hacerlo sin conocer el resultado. La defensa personal es el primer paso para asegurar respeto entre las instituciones de violencia, el estado y las personas. Antes de borrarlas tenemos que ser respetados por el poder que poseemos en números e inteligencia. La responsabilidad colectiva tiene que surgir de abajo, de la confianza entre la gente, de la solidaridad y de la creencia compartida en la posibilidad de justicia.

Imagine un concepto de justicia basado en la curación en lugar del castigo. La comunidad rodea al culpable y se cuenta qué bien hizo esta persona además del acto delictivo hasta que la persona se siente parte de la comunidad nuevamente. Esto podría ser una base para la restauración de la confianza mutua y un sentido de justicia compartido colectivamente. Esto nunca será una dimensión de nuestra sociedad hasta que ganemos el respeto de los monopolistas.

ESTRATEGIAS DE ACCIÓN DURANTE Y DESPUÉS DE LA CUARENTENA:

- Mira desde tu balcón o ventana, cuida de tu vecindario y fíjate cómo son tratados por la policía en las calles.
- Participa en grupos y canales de comunicación que actúen a nivel de barrio o ciudad. Habla de responsabilidad colectiva con tu gente más cercana.
- Finalizada la cuarentena, interactúa con los grupos de apoyo a prisioneros, por ejemplo

- enviando libros, y únete al grupo antimilitarista o de autodefensa de tu ciudad.
- Nunca te alistes al ejército imperialista ni defiendas la guerra por el Estado o el capital..

EL FUTURO NO SE VENDE. NADIE SIN HOGAR, TODOS APÁTRIDAS. PENSAMIENTO GEOCENTRISTA QUE NOS SITÚE EN UNA ALDEA GLOBAL PARA TODOS.

CONTEXTO EN TIEMPOS DE CRISIS SANITARIA O ANTES:

Amanecer en estados de emergencia y toques de queda nos confronta con una sensación de libertad perdida. Nos hace pernoctar en nuestras viviendas, esos espacios estáticos en los que solemos desarrollar gran parte de nuestras vidas. Éstas a menudo resultan ser el único píxel del espacio vivido bajo nuestro control. El espacio remanente está gobernado por un modelo totalitarista de Estado y que la pandemia revela sus verdaderos defectos ante las necesidades básicas de sus habitantes en el mundo.

A lo largo de la historia, en los asentamientos que empezaban a crecer en habitantes, aumentaba el miedo a las pestes, lo que desencadenó en protocolos e instalaciones para proporcionar un aislamiento completo. La expulsión del "enfermo" fue total, como lo fue de la comunidad al exterior. Este sentido de control contribuyó a desarrollar la atracción hacia la posesión del 'espacio' o tierra donde uno o unos pocos tenían todo lo necesario. El desarrollo de bienes privados de nuestra sociedad posesiva también nos vendió muchas promesas de seguridad, estatus social y posibilidades económicas

Kuala Lumpur, Malasia 2018
Foto de
Alejandra Robles Sosa

para convertir la tierra en dinero.

La riqueza en tierras privadas les dio a algunos el poder para controlar y discriminar, lo que dividió los territorios y nos llevó a una fragmentación geopolítica surreal en la cual nos creemos dueños de una parte. Esa necesidad de controlar y sentirnos seguros en nuestras ciudades no nos garantiza los recursos necesarios para subsistir como ha demostrado la pandemia, entonces surgen la preguntas ¿qué es nuestro? y ¿de qué sirve el control sobre la tierra?

PROPUESTA:

No considerarse habitante de un hogar, ni de una ciudad, ni un país o territorio marcado por la diferencia. Pensar en un lugar donde uno pueda desarrollar su forma de vivir de manera grupal aceptando la diversidad y donde estemos dispuestos a cultivar lo colectivo antes de lo individual. Dejar el poder y la riqueza de la acumulación de lo innecesario por la abundancia del compartir nos devolverá el sentido de nuestras vidas compartidas, como las relaciones que formamos en grupo incluyendo a todos los seres del entorno en el que vivimos. Esta propuesta es la esencia de la injusticia ambiental en todas las escalas. La propiedad es un robo.

Los especuladores y grandes propietarios viven de la tierra que

es de todos. Crean dinero agregando valor de cambio artificial a un bien común que tiene un valor de uso infinito y que simplemente no puede ser mercantilizado. No debemos formar parte de este fraude económico sin sentido y, en cambio, debemos trabajar para facilitar la mayor cantidad posible de tierras y hogares a una gran parte de habitantes, incluidos los no humanos. La propiedad debe venir esencialmente con la responsabilidad compartida hacia la accesibilidad y reproducción del espacio y no con el privilegio de ganar dinero con el trabajo de otras personas. Toda la tierra es nuestra y toda la tierra puede administrarse como propiedad común. Todos los seres humanos necesitan un hogar y el hogar es más que un techo privado sobre nuestras cabezas privadas. Ese hogar puede construirse, mantenerse y poseerse como un espacio compartido de muchos propósitos para muchos usuarios con modelos como tierras comunitarias, esquemas de vivienda de autoayuda y devolver la tierra ocupada por sueños húmedos capitalistas como extensiones de aeropuertos, minas abiertas o urbanizaciones.

ESTRATEGIAS DE ACCIÓN DURANTE Y DESPUÉS DE LA CUARENTENA:

* Catalogar qué actividades hemos dejado de hacer y notar cuales dejaríamos porque ahora creemos que son innecesarias.
* Observar lo que no uso y qué le puede ser útil a otra persona para permitirnos desprendernos de aquello y compartirlo.
* Leer y comprender las injusticias de la tierra y la tenencia. La propiedad y la forma en que inscribe la injusticia en el espacio.
* Formar un grupo con nuestros amigos para discutir cómo queremos vivir cuando seamos viejos y cómo vemos nuestra visión del mundo en tierra de nadie.

Collage de
Alejandra Robles Sosa

Ilustraciones
Friedrich Losch
Varignana F. Mitelli

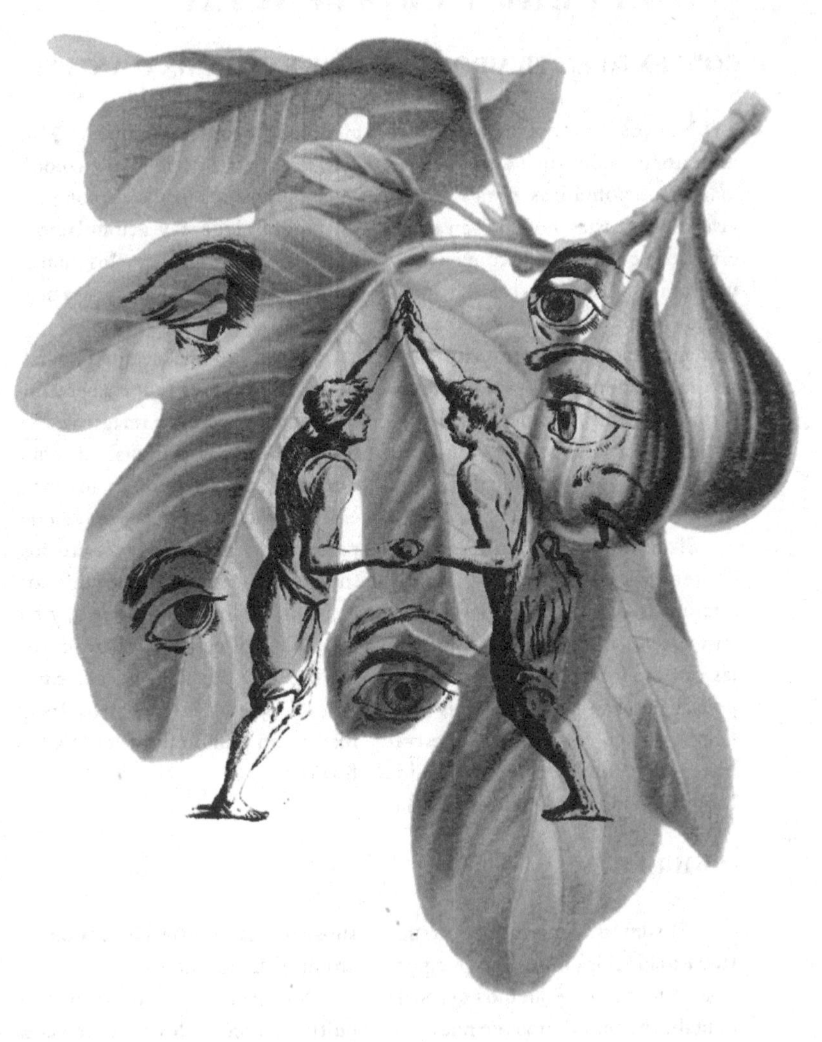

RE-TERRITORIALIZACIÓN Y LA RESISTENCIA CULTURAL INDÍGENA. RESPETE LA EXISTENCIA O ESPERE RESISTENCIA.

CONTEXTO EN TIEMPOS DE CRISIS SANITARIA O ANTES:

Nuevos atardeceres con aves migratorias que vuelven, escenas marinas espontáneas nunca antes vistas en las costas, nos vuelven a dar esperanza que podemos convivir en un mundo más inclusivo. La inesperada rehabilitación de los ecosistemas en nuestros entornos naturales, nos mantienen como espectadores de procesos que habíamos dejado de observar por la velocidad y nuestro apego a una vida individualista que siempre nos exige más.

Esta nueva oportunidad de contemplar el vacío y la disminución de movimiento que existe en nuestras ciudades sin que nadie las camine y las disfrute, nos hace pensar en el valor de las cosas que hemos ganado y perdido en nuestra historia personal y colectiva. Todo lo que hemos construido en la civilización contemporánea se basa en una idolatría occidental y colonial sujeta por una visión de conquista, rápida riqueza y acumulación. Alguien merece más que los demás porque trabaja, explota o saquea más duro.

Es por eso que, según Thomas Moore, la utopía es la única herramienta que nos permite imaginar. No olvidemos que hoy en día, así como durante gran parte de la historia, existen sociedades indígenas que preservan y mantienen territorios, integrando a su modo de vida los ciclos naturales y los saberes, y en las que aún podemos confiar y cuyos modos aún podemos revaloricemos antes de que los estropeemos. Imaginamos un mundo de acuerdo a sus formas.

PROPUESTA:

El sometimiento a una estructura establecida omite otras perspectivas e historias. Podemos desoccidentalizar cómo vivimos en nuestros territorios y descolonizar cómo nos relacionamos con otras sociedades indígenas y las formas de habitar la Tierra, ya que el modo de vida capitalista actual ha determinado la subsistencia en este planeta en un absolutismo totalitario.

Nuestras civilizaciones y culturas ancestrales muchas veces se basaron en conocimientos y creencias que valoran holísticamente a los seres de la Tierra, ya sean plantas o animales, por lo que mantuvieron un conocimiento de

vivir en armonía con el medio ambiente durante miles de años. Y gran parte de esta memoria la conservan las sociedades indígenas de todo el mundo. Nosotros, que fracasamos en esto, tenemos que considerar la importancia de la convivencia del ser humano y su hábitat, y la empatía por el otro, respetando la lucha por recuperar el sentido de pertenencia a todos aquellos nacimientos que despojamos del futuro hace mucho tiempo. Porque la convivencia está, como sabían nuestros ancestros y antecesores nativos, no inscrita en el mapa, sino en flujos cíclicos vitales de la vida terrenal.

ESTRATEGIAS DE ACCIÓN DURANTE Y DESPUÉS DE LA CUARENTENA:

- Conocer el significado del término descolonizar y apoyar el movimiento de los pueblos indígenas hacia su autonomía.
- Pensar menos en nosotros mismos y en lo que echamos de menos, y hacer un esfuerzo por cuidar lo que hemos heredado.
- Relajarse y hacer una introspección para reconocer de qué seres vivimos rodeados. Ver cuán similares y diferentes somos a ellos y cuánto estamos dispuestos a compartir con todo lo que nos rodea.

Ecuador 2017
Foto de
Alejandra Robles Sosa

"Cuando sueñas solo,
sólo es un sueño;
cuando sueñas con otros,
es el comienzo de la realidad"

Proverbio Brasileño

"When you dream alone, it is
just a dream. When you dream
with others it is the beginning
of reality"

Brazilian proverb